MAGIC
—— Sarah Foot ——
& Michael Williams

Thank you for all you do
for the cats.

1,000 Thanks.

Best wishes.

Michael Williams.

Land's End
St Just

May 2007

BOSSINEY BOOKS

First published in 1995
by Bossiney Books, St Teath, Bodmin, Cornwall

Typeset and printed by Penwell Ltd, Callington, Cornwall

© Sarah Foot and Michael Williams

ISBN 1 899383 00 X

ACKNOWLEDGEMENTS

Front cover photograph: Roy Westlake
Front cover design: Maggie Ginger
Back cover photography: Roy Westlake
Other photographs: Ray Bishop, Michael Deering, Dermot
FitzGerald, S Ryder, George WF Ellis,
Sharpe's Studios, PEC Smith, Murray
King, Woolf-Greenham, Bernard
Mottram, Alice Lennox-Boyd

3

MICHAEL WILLIAMS, a Cornishman, started full-time publishing in 1975. He and his wife Sonia live in a cottage on the shoulder of a green valley just outside St Teath in North Cornwall.

In addition to publishing and writing, Michael Williams is a keen cricketer and collector of cricket books and autographs. He was the first captain of the Cornish Crusaders Cricket Club and is today President of the Crusaders. He is also a member of Cornwall and Gloucestershire County Cricket Clubs – and a Vice-President of the Cornwall Rugby Football Union. A member of the International League for the Protection of Horses and the RSPCA, he has worked hard for reform in laws relating to animal welfare.

Locally he is a patron of the Broomfield Horse Sanctuary at Trewellard.

He is a member of the Ghost Club Society, and is their representative in the south west. His latest publication was **Edge of the Unknown** *investigating a wide range of paranormal cases in the Westcountry, many appearing in book form for the first time.*

Outside his Bossiney activities, Michael has recently set up as a writing and publishing consultant, evaluating manuscripts and advising writers.

Here in Bossiney's 230th title he collaborates with Sarah Foot exploring **Magical Places:** *a tour in words and pictures of favourite locations in Cornwall and Devon, 'places that seem to be touched by magic of some kind'.*

MAGICAL PLACES

MAGICAL places. Do such locations really exist? Or are they only to be found in the eye of our imagination? That faithful old friend *Collins English Dictionary* devotes ten sections – ten definitions – to the word *magic*. We like references to 'the magic of spring' and 'unaccountably enchanting.'

And, of course, the word crops up again and again in the supernatural field. Magic in this supernatural sense, I suppose, is defined as the means whereby we can discover unknown powers of nature and the *using* of those powers. And some of the locations on this tour of the west may come into that category, haunted, but they will be in the minority. So perhaps we need to go to that great Dorset writer to get to the heart of our brand of magic.

Thomas Hardy came in search of the elusive spirit of Cornwall, and many years later he wrote:

When I came back from Lyonesse
With magic in my eyes,
All marked with mute surprise
My radiance rare and fathomless,
When I came back from Lyonesse
With magic in my eyes.

But we are sensible enough to know magic does not end at the western bank of the River Tamar. Devon, too, has its own – a different kind of magic maybe – but still beguiling.

More than fifty years ago Arthur Mee asked: 'What do they know of England who do not know Devon?' Naturally there has been massive development in Devon since Mr Mee wrote those words and Devon can never be confused with Cornwall. Nevertheless

6

GRIMSPOUND. In an early and now out of print Bossiney title James Turner wrote 'Dartmoor is so large that you cannot take it all in, as you can Bodmin Moor, in one or two visits. You return to places which attract you. Such a place is Grimspound, one of the most open and most haunted parts of the moor'.

Devon remains English to the core: the towns, the seaports, the lovely villages and, above all, the awe and majesty of Dartmoor – and a great deal more.

I recall an interview with that brilliant wordsmith Ronald Duncan in his farmhouse kitchen up by the Cornwall Devon border near Morwenstow.

'To move from one house to another is more than changing our address,' he told me. 'We think it merely a matter of shifting the furniture, buying new curtains and finding new tradesmen...we unpack our books and assume our personality will impose itself on our new surroundings. *That* is where we make a big mistake. It is not we who change a house, but the house which changes us...'

Later – much later – I recalled the wisdom of Ronald's words, and recalled them in a wider, more important, sense.

Certain places have changed me. To quote two obvious examples, without coming to terms with first Bodmin Moor and later, Dartmoor, I would have grown into a different, a poorer Cornishman. One may be in Cornwall, the other in Devon, and they may possess different personalities but they belong to the same tribe. Two very different painters, Charles Simpson, a traditional landscape painter and Peter Lanyon, an internationally famous modern, in their contrasting ways taught me the landscape is not something we simply see, but something we live in and experience.

Our south westerly landscapes are full of richness and subtle quality – and we must remember there are wide varieties in the terrain: from hills and tors to secret valleys and brooding moorland under wide skies, from dark woods to the coast and the open sea.

In travel, whatever the scale, we need to be receptive. By absorbing ourselves into the experience of the journey – or the destination – we somehow blend into the surroundings and accept what

YOU cannot go far in Cornwall and not be touched by King Arthur. Here are the ruins of Tintagel Castle on an old picture postcard posted in Boscastle in 1910.

The Ruins, Tintagel Castle.
Photo R. Weber

8

comes. That anyway has been my way and, as a result, we become part of the landscape – and that is where the real reward comes.

Getting back to Ronald Duncan he was an extraordinary man – gifted in various literary fields: poet and playwright, autobiographer and short story writer, film critic and essayist. He once described himself as 'an animated inkblot'. Ezra Pound referred to him as 'the lone wolf of English letters'. Often he looked like a Devonshire tramp – and was rather proud of the fact – yet he had a fatal attraction for beautiful younger women. I didn't meet him more than a few times, but he made a tremendous impact, and was a valued contributor to the Bossiney list in our early days. Our first meeting was for an interview feature in the *Cornish Review*. After conversation over coffee, we walked out to his writer's hut on the cliffs and he told me '...the storms and gales we get along this coast make comments with which I agree'.

He opened my eyes to the beauty and the cruelty of this coastline. I never come to the Morwenstow area without thinking of him.

My co-author and I have no wish to become a nun or monk, but we can understand how, in this busy bustling life, people can be drawn to the calm of the cloister. Modern life does unleash feverish, oppressive demands – and on some of these journeys we have found release and refreshment. More than once, too, we have remembered the Holy Grail and understood that Arthur is all about a quest for our better self or selves. You cannot go far in this region without being touched by the spirit of Camelot.

Come then, let us begin our tour of *Magical Places*. And where better to begin than the Lizard?

◄ *A PAINTER can alter our vision. I am grateful to Cornish painters who have sharpened my awareness of both land and seascape. One of my favourite native painters is Jack Pender, member of a well-known Mousehole family. Here is a Jack Pender painting dating from the 1960s. In an interview around that time he said 'My window looks out on to two granite quays enclosing a small harbour with a wide vista of sea and sky beyond. I am constantly aware of the interplay of space and solid, shape and colour, and of the relationship of boat to boat, to quay, to sea and to man'.*

GUNWALLOE AND KENNACK SANDS ON THE LIZARD

THE LIZARD is a unique corner of Cornwall: Britain's farthest south. Lizard is the heel of Cornwall, whereas Land's End is the toe and Mount's Bay the sole. For some people the peninsula can be a new beginning – for others the end of the world, as indeed it was, for this coastline is littered with wrecks. Layers of history and legend cloak the land and the sea hereabouts.

Yes, rich in history. The Spanish Armada sailed on the Lizard sea. The Armada came up from the south on a July afternoon in 1588; observers on The Rill saw the invaders coming and warning beacons flared quickly along the Cornish coast. The theatre critic JC Trewin, who contributed an early Bossiney chapter, recalled his father pointing and saying 'There boy – that's where the Dons came up from southward'.

That fine travel writer Lady Clara Vyvyan, who lived for many years at Trelowarren, once said: 'If I were asked to describe the country briefly, I should use the single word *magic*'.

The cliffs, the ever-changing sea and the rocks; the bird life and the wild flowers; the moorland space and, at certain times, the clarity of the light: Lizard has many qualities. This is the serpentine peninsula and the predominant colour of the serpentine is an olive green.

One of my favourite Cornish churches is Gunwalloe. A remote building hunched against a small rocky headland, Gunwalloe is a beautiful unexpected sight. I try to visit Gunwalloe at least twice a year because it has a peace which passes most understandings: a perfect place for meditation. The sea washes its walls; the biggest waves fly over it.

A former Vicar, the Rev Frederick William Marshall told me: 'I

11

go down to Gunwalloe almost every day and very often I'm conscious of something deeply spiritual there. I've never seen anything, but I've many times felt surrounded by the departed. At service when I say "The Lord be with thy spirit," I get a response beyond the number of those present. The odour of past prayer hangs about the place.'

'The glory of a building,' wrote Ruskin, 'is in its age, and in that deep sense of voicefulness, of stern watching, of mysterious sympathy, nay, even of approval or condemnation which we feel in walls that have been washed by humanity.' He could have been writing about this lovely old church by the sea.

On the other side of the peninsula is one of my favourite beaches. Kennack Sands are curiously underwritten. Time and again I have turned to a new book on Cornwall – new to me anyway – and found no mention of these twin sandy beaches. They can be a tonic. I invariably come away feeling a different, a better person. These lines are being written at St Teath in North Cornwall on a grey wet and misty December afternoon. Close by on one of my library shelves are two pebbles from Kennack Sands. Spirits lift.

It was Dame Daphne du Maurier who first told me about Kennack Sands. 'I taught myself to swim there,' she reflected recalling childhood memories of Cornwall. 'But to me, even then, the sea seemed cruel, demanding victims.'

12

GUNWALLOE CHURCH, pictured left, overlooks this lovely beach. On the left is the former Poldhu Hotel, now a retirement home. On the cliffs beyond the hotel is the spot where Marconi sent his historic radio messages across the Atlantic.

When Sonia and I were staying at the Polrurrian Hotel at Mullion, I met an American geologist who told me 'Kennack has four different rock types, all within yards of each other'. He thought it 'a Klondike'. Other visitors in the hotel enthused about places like St Ives, Land's End and the ruins of Tintagel Castle, but Kennack Sands had made *his* visit to Cornwall.

I prefer the sands out of season. In fact I've never been here in July or August when our Cornish beaches are busy, bustling with the noise of children and their buckets and spades – and good luck to them: Cornish tourism needs them and their parents. I have been here in winter, undeterred by what we foolishly call 'bad weather', days when JMW Turner, the greatest of British painters, would have produced some of his most atmospheric art. Turner did spend a spell in Cornwall. I wonder if anyone told him about Kennack Sands.

THE PAINTING CHEMISTRY OF LAMORNA

CORNWALL'S ability to fire creativity has a long and distinguished history. It's a curious fact that *some* Cornish places – sometimes quite small areas – have generated a remarkable amount of writing and painting, potting and sculpting. Lamorna is such a place.

The explanation though is elusive.

First, there is the natural beauty of the valley and the cove. Perhaps creative characters, like painters and writers, follow in the footsteps of others. I'm less sure about that word 'colony'. One eminent Lamorna painter John Tunnard once reprimanded me: 'You writers get it all wrong, talking about "colonies". Many of us work in total isolation … Just a matter between the painter and his piece of canvas.'

Charles Simpson, a fine painter and writer, who lived for a while at Lamorna, said: 'It's a congenial place, lots of visual qualities but I honestly don't know why or how it's produced so much, maybe the brilliance of the light'. Denys Law, who lived and painted in the valley for many years told me: 'I don't think one can put a finger on it, not exactly anyway. It's a unique valley, it changes, yes, but there's something … something almost unworldly about it.'

So, in a way, Lamorna defies neat easy classification.

There is no doubt, though, that one painter, above all others, will be identified with this valley of varying moods and colours. Samuel John Birch may have hailed from Cheshire, but from 1892 until his death in 1955 – apart from a year in Paris – he was an essential part of the Lamorna landscape and coastline. A brilliant talent with oils and watercolours, his vision owed much to the rain-washed and

'LAMORNA' BIRCH painting in oils. This painting was a gift from Cornwall to Princess Elizabeth on the occasion of her wedding.

sometimes misty scenery of Britain and Cornwall in particular. But due to the French influences, painters like Monet and Pissarro, his landscapes can glow with colour. A master with running water, he was also deeply sensitive to light and its effect. A considerable naturalist, his respect for nature frequently shone from his pictures. His trees, in particular, have a living quality – you start seeing them as personalities in their own right.

His adoption of the name Lamorna was the result of confusion with another painter Lionel Birch. Often they received each other's mail, and it was Stanhope Forbes of Newlyn who solved the problem, saying 'We'll call you Lamorna Birch!'

The distinguished Sir Alfred Munnings had links with Lamorna. Known locally as 'the man who could really paint a horse', he lived for a while at The Wink, the inn by the stream. He hung paintings on the walls there and exhibited in the Newlyn gallery. It was here

LAMORNA by John Birch on an old picture postcard.

in Cornwall that he met his first wife Florence, and it was Florence who fired his first attempt to paint a sophisticated lady on horseback. The result, Florence elegantly mounted sidesaddle on a splendid bay, entitled 'The Morning Ride' gave him great personal satisfaction.

But the success of that painting almost certainly blinded him to the unsuitability of their marriage. It began with disaster and ended with disaster: a marriage he totally ignored in his later autobiography. Florence finally committed suicide in what is today the Lamorna Cove Hotel.

There were other Lamorna painters like the Knights, Dame Laura and her husband Harold, and Ernest Procter, and we must not forget people like Frank Heath, Robert and Eleanor Hughes, Charles Naper and Stanley Gardiner. The fact that such talented characters lived and worked here or had 'a Lamorna phase' speaks

LAMORNA COVE, painted in oils by Lamorna Kerr, daughter of John Birch.

volumes for the creative chemistry.

But John Birch was the presiding spirit. He, more than anybody else, understood the beauty and the subtleties of Lamorna – and lovingly pinned them to canvas and in watercolour.

Birch may be gone. Yet in another sense he has never left the place, living on in his work. Whenever I come to this lovely corner of West Cornwall I half expect to see a short bearded figure at his easel.

*   *   *   *   *

LAND'S END

JUST two words, but how they fire our imagination. The views from Land's End are magnificent. My simple advice is merely walk a furlong or two either right or left, and you will understand words cannot do them justice.

If you will make that effort then you will be rewarded by some of the finest coastal scenery in all Britain – some people would say some of the finest anywhere in the world. The cliffs are spectacular and their colouring vivid: on a crystal clear day golden and grey cliffs seen against an emerald sea.

As a young man on one of my first visits, I remember – remember as if it were last evening – experiencing something almost unworldly, something deeper than the dramatic beauty and the red sky at sunset.

For more than thirty years I have been investigating the paranormal, and Land's End carries many supernatural echoes. According to one version, the figure of a man once stood on the point and a prophetic tradition persisted to the effect that it would fall on a day of some great disaster – the Celts have always believed in signs and omens – and the figure did just that on the thirtieth day of January 1649, the date on which King Charles was beheaded. Furthermore, almost as if to underline the eerie fact, on that same day a vessel, carrying the King's treasure and furniture, broke from its moorings and was wrecked at Godrevy in St Ives Bay. Not one curious coincidence, but two.

DR Johnson's Head. ▶

18

19

Inevitably Land's End means different things to different people.

For many it is a pilgrimage – for many a lifelong ambition – for others it will be Lyonesse or Arthur or both. Outside and beyond these are the physical qualities: the granite boulders and the sea, the sky and, on the right kind of day, the brilliant Penwith light which has been such a factor in so many fine paintings. The names hereabouts stir our curiosity: Dr Syntax, the Armed Knight, Dr Johnson's Head, the Irish Lady ... no ordinary place. There is the realization that you're following in famous footsteps. Richard Carew in the early 1600s at the end of his Survey of Cornwall reflected 'We are arrived. I will here sit mee downe and rest.'

The Land's End peninsula and the Isles of Scilly have been Britain's first landfall for generations of homecoming seamen. Variously known as the Western Approaches or, to the old sea dogs, 'Chops of the Channel', this area has more recently been christened 'the Celtic Sea' – and maybe this modern title rings truest of all.

For generations coastal dwellers have laboured on these changing waters, their origins rooted deeply in the creeks and inlets. The atmosphere of the long ago lives on among the granite of this beautiful but wicked coastline.

For me a visit to Land's End is always a worthwhile experience – and a new beginning.

* * * * *

AN OLD picture postcard. The sender writes 'Oh dear, we are late for the coach … always late, that's us!'

VIEW from Land's End – Cape Cornwall in the distance.

RUGBY action at Redruth – Cornwall 22, Somerset 3: November 1985.

RUGBY
AT REDRUTH

Rugby in Cornwall is almost a religion – many people would say it *is* a religion. There is a tremendous atmosphere at Redruth on county championship match days. I have watched games on many Westcountry grounds, but know of no other which equals the unique atmosphere of Redruth. Hellfire Corner has become part of the folklore of the game.

DR Gent, who played for Gloucester and England and went on to become one of the finest writers in Rugby history, has called it 'This glorious game, glorious mainly because it is so vigorous … no game brings out all that is best in man so effectively as Rugby football does.'

It may sound old-fashioned, but I really believe games, like Rugby and cricket, are character-building. The social aspect of sport alone adds to the quality of life.

On a county match afternoon this recreation ground at Redruth becomes a cauldron and that atmosphere somehow electrifies the game. Few teams can relish tackling Cornwall here before a big crowd. 'Bonzo' Johns, who played 88 times for Cornwall, was a Barbarian and an England trialist. He told me 'That roar makes you give everything you've got'.

I have also talked to Ken Williams, who played for Redruth from 1928 to 1938, about the Redruth slope. 'From the north-east to the south-west there's a gradual slope of about four feet … yes, there's this very intensive atmosphere at Redruth. I think it's largely due to the fact that the spectators are very much closer to the actual playing pitch than on many grounds.'

Recently I unearthed some old newspaper cuttings, yellowing

23

with age and written more than thirty years ago. Here is something I wrote on this ground all those years ago for the *Cornishman:* 'I am writing these lines on November 14 – Cornwall v Devon – in a few minutes these ancient rivals will emerge from the tunnel below me, and yet another local derby will be underway. I arrived at the ground almost an hour ago – not even a burst of torrential rain has dampened the electricity of the atmosphere.

'As I write one can feel the tension building up. One can readily appreciate that for the players who are making their debuts this afternoon, these last nerve-racking minutes in the dressing-rooms below are emotion-charged, probably more taxing than anything that will be encountered on the actual playing pitch.

'In front of the grandstand, a local band plays its traditional part, but it is only background music … there is a general hub of con-versation. "Who will win? If we do, are you going to Gloucester? Cornwall are favourites today – is that a bad thing? When did Devon last win here?"

'But, here and there, one spots an old player not speaking. His eyes are on the pitch. Perhaps he is going back in time to some match or some moment that now belongs to the history book and his own store of memories.'

It was on this ground in 1908 that Cornwall beat Durham in the final of the county championship – we had to wait another 83 years to win it a second time and I was lucky enough to be at Twickenham to see Cornwall do it.

Yes, great deeds have taken place on this Redruth ground, and I have long felt the magic owes something to the past: the spirit of historic games past merging into the present.

*   *   *   *   *

THE
ROSELAND

THE ROSELAND, like the Lizard, is a world of its own. There is a very Cornish quality abut the names of this area: Gerrans and Portscatho, Veryan and Trelissa, Greeb and Treluggan are only some of them.

As for the name Roseland, when John Norden, the celebrated map maker from Somerset, came to Cornwall in the 1580s, he wrote 'The peninsula is called by the pretty name of Roseland which has however nothing to do with flowers, being derived from Rhos, the Celtic word for heath or gorse'.

For me the jewel in Roseland's crown is the church of St Just-in-Roseland. Here in this romantic setting by water, we come face to face with a great Cornish mystery and question. Did Christ, as a boy, come to Cornwall?

There is a legend, bordering on a mixture of hope and belief, that the young Jesus did precisely that. There are various versions but the basic story is Jesus came to Cornwall with Joseph of Arimathea on a tin-buying venture. It is believed Joseph was an uncle of Mary, the mother of Jesus. Joseph was more than a trader and merchant, he was a skilful sailor and navigator. So it was natural he should suggest the boy Jesus should come with him on one of his voyages. And, of course, it is historically possible.

After all, Blake, the mystic, wrote those stirring words:
And did those Feet in ancient time
Walk upon England's mountains green
And was the Holy Lamb of God
On England's pleasant pastures seen?
Jane Oliver, in a book entitled *In No Strange Land*, published back

25

SOWING barley near Veryan on the Roseland.

in the 1940s, makes Joseph on a later visit say: 'He loved the country and its little creatures. I always knew that he saw every stirring thing, though I, may I be forgiven, tried to turn his mind to the business through which I had made my wealth. But he only smiled at my talk of ingots and miners' wages. The fishermen now, he was far more interested in them.' That certainly is a word picture which will appeal to all who cherish the Christ in Cornwall theory.

But, alas, as with Arthur we lack any reliable written record.

There are, of course, intriguing links. Arthur's quest for the Holy Grail is central to the whole Arthurian theme, and legend maintains that the Chalice, used by Christ at the Last Supper, was brought to this country by the same Joseph of Arimathea.

Times were when I saw fact and legend inside clearly defined areas, but the older I get the less certain I become about the clarity of some definitions. Indeed I seriously doubt whether there be any total myth, no shred of reality. Smoke without fire?

Wallace Nichols, the poet and novelist who lived in the Penzance area for many years, was interested in the Christ in Cornwall theme to such an extent he wrote about it. In my library I have an autographed copy of his Dramatic Morality in Two Acts, entitled *The Boy from Egypt*. Wallace Nichols, who had a vivid imagination (he claimed the Pope blessed it on a visit to the Vatican) was nevertheless a stickler for accuracy. In one of our last conversations at

Usticke Haven, on the outskirts of Penzance, Wallace explained 'The work is based on a persistent rumour which has run in Cornwall for centuries. It's a symbolic drama with roots in legend … but the whole thing is historically feasible.'

I must not give the impression Roseland is only St Just-in-Roseland. St Mawes, with its castle, is a much loved resort for many people. Nearby, Place, a fascinating mixture of private house and church, reputedly visited by Henry VIII, dominates beautiful St Anthony-in-Roseland. Portscatho is one of my wife Sonia's favourite villages, an open spot on low cliffs, looking mainly eastward and out of the wind. These are only a few worthwhile Roseland destinations.

And, of course, the peninsula boasts an outstanding hotel. The Nare Hotel, above Carne Beach near Veryan, stands in extensive ground surrounded by National Trust land with wide views of Gerrans Bay and Nare Head from which it derives its name.

In 1993 The Nare achieved four star rating from the RAC and the AA, becoming the highest rated four star hotel in Devon and Cornwall. The sub-tropical climate and caring professional staff make it a popular choice any time in the year.

DAFFODIL time on the Roseland.

LERRYN

I HAVE been writing about Cornwall for more than forty years, but by some curious twist of fate or conscious choice, I have never written a sentence about a favourite place.

Sonia urged me to rectify the matter in this, our 230th Bossiney title.

Lerryn is a magical location, a quiet estuary village, but, like Kennack Sands down on the Lizard, it is a strangely underwritten part of Kernow. There are two Lerryns: one when the tide is in and the trees bend down to touch the water like supple ballerinas and another when the tide is out and the shiny mud is revealed. I have been here in good weather and bad, and never been disappointed.

Of course, when the sun shines and there is a sparkle in the water, Lerryn has a special dimension. We brought a couple from London here one Sunday afternoon – we had lunched at the Fowey Hotel – and the husband, who had not been well, later said to me 'That Lerryn was better than any medicine or therapy!'

There are some interesting associations with Lerryn. Eric Portman, the actor, lived here, and the author Kenneth Grahame walked along the riverside path when staying at Fowey. Some say his classic the *Wind in the Willows* owed something to Lerryn and district. It's that kind of place, firing the imagination and stirring our curiosity.

I remember coming to Lerryn to look at some horse paintings by Peter Howell, who had worked for eminent racehorse trainers like Toby Baldwin and Fulke Walwyn. The long tough hours of working in racing stables never dimmed Peter's enthusiasm for art; in fact they proved to be a kind of valuable preparatory school for his

career as a painter. A Peter Howell painting is more than horse and rider. The thoroughbred may be the focal point of his painting but it is subtle colouring, skilful use of light and understanding of the landscape that make his work so vivid and vital.

Nearby is the Giant's Hedge which has a special place in the folklore of Cornwall. Some say it's among the Devil's best architecture, and they quote an ancient rhyme which runs:

'The Devil having nothing to do,
Built a great wall from Lerryn to Looe.'

The pure historian will have none of this, insisting it's just a fortification built in the sixth century by King Mark to keep out the attacking Irish. But some of the older folk shake their heads, standing by that ancient belief in the Devil.

It was the author Denys Val Baker who first introduced me to Lerryn and the surrounding countryside and waterways. He was then living at the Old Sawmills at Golant, and often sailed up to Lerryn. Denys was not only a talented literary all-rounder, he gave me some wonderful writing opportunities for his *Cornish Review*, and encouraged me to venture into publishing. Sonia and I were then at Bossiney, Sir Francis Drake's old constituency hard by Tintagel on the north coast, and, over dinner one evening he said 'Your company can have only one name: Bossiney Books'. He was rarely dogmatic but he was absolutely certain this should be our name.

At Lerryn we are not far from the smugglers' haunts of Polperro. Cornish smugglers did not see themselves as members of the criminal class. They rated themselves 'fair traders', and all layers of Cornish society were involved, the gentry buying their wine and spirits at 'cut' prices and, on occasion, Customs House men conniving. But we must not overromanticise the smugglers and their work: deeds frequently stained with murder and corruption, treachery and violence.

The smugglers had the foresight to advise local people when their contingent travelled through the village or hamlet, they

THE quiet estuary village of Lerryn.

should face the wall. Consequently if smugglers were arrested the villagers could, with hands on heart, say '*We saw nothing*'.

'Them that ask no questions isn't told a lie, watch the wall, my darling, while the gentlemen go by ... '

More than forty years ago John Betjeman – later Sir John and Poet Laureate – on a visit to Ethy, a late Georgian manor, wrote 'In the valley below is Lerryn with its boats, cottages and Methodist chapel and inn looking like a feudal dependency of Ethy, but actually an independent place mostly in the parish of St Veep'.

If Sir John came back, he would be pleased to know much of the beauty and healing quality remain.

LOOKING up the North Cornish cliffs from a point near Trevalga. This is one of my favourite stretches of coastline in all Cornwall.

LESNEWTH, one of North Cornwall's loveliest and least photographed churches.

TREVALGA
and LESNEWTH

HAVING lived at Bossiney for a decade, I have a special affection for the Tintagel district. One of my favourite spots is Trevalga. This hamlet is a gem: an unspoilt corner of North Cornwall.

The literary JD Cook, the founder and editor of the *Saturday Review*, who was born at Camelford and is remembered in Tintagel Church, lived at Trevalga. The real joy of the place is that a former Lord of the Manor had a generous and inspired idea. Mr Gerald Curgenven, who had been educated at Marlborough College in Wiltshire and later taught at Clifton College, on the death of his wife had no family or close relatives. His love for Trevalga was such that he made special provisions in his will to ensure the village and the Manor would be kept in the same character. So as long as Marlborough prospers, Trevalga will be safe from the developers.

The church, dedicated to St Petroc, stands more or less in a farmyard. But the saint would not have minded, for he was a true Celt, being half Welsh and half Irish and understanding the countryside. Back in the 1970s when I was RSPCA Secretary for this area, we held an animal service here which attracted an incredible variety of animals and television cameras. St Petroc was a great apostle of Devon and Cornwall. He founded a community at Padstow before moving on to Bodmin, the religious capital of Cornwall down to the end of the Middle Ages. Many stories are told about this wonderful man who is reputed to have been kind to dragons!

The church building is interesting in that there are traces of Norman work in the lower masonry. The narrow nave has a tiny chapel reached by a Norman arch, and the font was shaped by a

Norman craftsman out of local greenstone. There is a piscina, a stone basin used for rinsing the chalice, and a peephole which enabled people sitting in the side chapel to see the action at the altar.

If you are interested in church art, there is plenty to see. There is a Dutch carving in the dark wood with scenes depicting the Visitation, the Annunciation and the Crucifixion. As many as twenty characters people three panels: Mary seen under a canopy speaking to Gabriel and God despatching a dove from the sky, while behind the figures of Mary and Elizabeth are two charming Dutch houses; and in the Crucifixion section John, in company with the two Marys, is seen at the foot of the cross. Four angels hold chalices at the nailed feet and hands.

There is some really noble woodwork, much of it given by Bolitho Stephens in his time as Lord of the Manor. The pulpit, shaped by Exeter carvers, is to his memory, as are the sanctuary chair and desk, all of which were donated by his widow in November 1929. The pulpit shows chapters in the career of St Petroc. Notice the Saint with his stag, and with his sheepskin and staff protected by a wolf; again an angel awakes him with the command to go to Brittany. In the small panels is a delicate carving of a ship fully rigged. There is, too, an east window with pictures of the Adoration of the Kings, the Annunciation and the Ascension. Arthur Mee was not exaggerating when he said 'Trevalga has still an art gallery worth looking at'.

Outside in the churchyard there is an aged moss-coated cross, standing some five feet and eight inches; and, of course, there are superlative views of the Atlantic and the cliffs merging into a memorable picture.

Trevalga is a great edge of the ocean experience. I have seen sunsets at Land's End and Trevalga and they are both in the same breathtaking league. Here we face the open Atlantic: nothing between us and North America. Magical is the only word.

A lane leads from the hamlet out to a strange 'terrace' of heather-peppered cliffs. If you have walked from Tintagel over the cliffs to Boscastle, you will know words can convey only a fraction of the drama and beauty. If you have not, then you have missed a rich experience, for hereabouts is one of the finest coastlines in all

Britain. Lady's Window is a curious rock formation 'a perforated rocky crag sharply silhouetted against the sky'.

Provided you have a head for heights you may be tempted to step through the narrow – very narrow – ledge and look down some 200 feet to the sea. Trevethet Gutt too is a lovely creek, and is probably best seen from a boat.

There are some places which seem almost untouched by time. Lesnewth is one such location. I first discovered it in 1965 and went again recently – in January 1995 to be precise – and in all those thirty years the countryside has scarcely changed.

The lane from Minster to Lesnewth is a delight – unless you happen to be a motorist in a hurry – Sir John Betjeman called it 'sylvan'. Twisting and turning, rising and falling, forever narrow, it takes you through the little hamlet of Treword and, at points, crosses streams. At any time in the year, this is one of the most delightful walks in the whole of North Cornwall.

The poets have waxed lyrical about spring and autumn, but I have a special liking for January, the beginning of a new year, the bustle and the emotions of Christmas behind us. So I was pleased to go back to Lesnewth on a January morning. Yesterday was a fine day, and Sonia, driving back from Plymouth, remarked how the days seemed to be lengthening: nothing dramatic but just a few minutes. May be the fact that I have an Aquarian birthday in January has something to do with it. Anyway, a good time for turning the pages of books, enjoying fires and looking to the future – and finishing my half of *Magical Places*.

Lesnewth stands at the head of a quiet wooded valley. Like nearby Minster, this Church of St Michael and All Angels was built in a dip. Prior to Norman times, it was a custom to build churches inland in the hope of avoiding Scandinavian invaders; we therefore find these older churches strategically tucked away in the countryside and the later buildings, after the Norman Conquest, occupying more exposed positions by the coast.

In Cornwall we attach a supernatural quality to St Michael in that he appeared to fishermen at St Michael's Mount in Mount's Bay, West Cornwall on the eighth day of May 495, when the island was home to hermits and anchorites – and, of course, he has a special role west of the Tamar as a guardian.

There is a peace here in both the church and the churchyard, ideal for anyone seeking a prescription for 'the strange disease called modern life' as Patrick Leigh Fermor put it. The troubled waters of the 1990s mind can grow still and clear and, after a while, the humble pilgrim can attain a peace that is generally unthought of in the thing we call the ordinary world.

The word Lesnewth means new court, and was possibly so-called when it became the capital of a sub-division of the ancient Hundred of Trigg in Saxon days. Again, like Minster, there are links across the Channel. A member of the Pomeroy family gave the right of appointing a Rectory to the Abbey of Val in Normandy which, in 1237, sold it to Henry de Daneys, reserving a princely pension of five shillings. It is believed that the first church was erected by the Saxons. Despite its cleverly concealed geography, the church had the ill-luck to be spotted by marauding Danes who pillaged it on their way to sack Manor Helsey.

The second church, built by the Normans, was cruciform in shape. Again like neighbouring Minster, it fell into depressing dilapidation, and in 1862 the ruthless JP St Aubyn presided over its restoration. Parts of the original incorporated into the present building are the three-pointed doorway and a Norman altar slab over the sill of the north window in the chancel. Dynamite was used in the demolition, and fragments of the old church can be seen sunken into the hedge, south west of the tower. Lesnewth, like so many North Cornish churches, suffered badly from drastic restoration. The restorers, in their enthusiasm, destroyed so many good things, but few people regretted the disappearance of the old-fashioned pew boxes.

In this context, AJ Beresford Hope, MP, told an amusing story at the re-opening of Lesnewth in 1866. ' ... a church having been restored, where the Squire of the Parish thinking himself a fine fellow, said the church was good enough for farmers and shopkeepers, and he would not have his gallery taken down. The church was restored in a very beautiful manner, only that abominable cage in which the Squire sat was retained. When the church was opened, the Squire, who thought he had done a very clever thing, went up to the principal farmer saying " ... Mr Jones, you see I have stuck to my old pew; what do people say of me?" Jones scratched his head and repeated the question … "Well, sir, if you will have me to tell you, they say you look like a jackass in a horsebox!"'

Outside, standing above the stream which passes through the churchyard and near the white railed footbridge is another good example of a Celtic cross. This one is said to have stood originally at Waterpit Down. A curate suggested that it should be resurrected here, but a local farmer, on whose land it had lain for some time, thought otherwise. He wanted to use it as a pig's trough.

MICHAEL Williams has a distant view of Dartmoor.

DARTMOOR

DARTMOOR is an energising experience. It is a landscape of contrast and varying mood. Even today from certain angles it can seem as remote as the moon. With its tawny manelike colouring, Dartmoor is quite unlike anywhere else in the Westcountry – or the British Isles.

This last wilderness spreads itself across 365 square miles. Here you meet the largest mass of granite in the kingdom. More than ten rivers make their way across it.

Back in the 1960s I was doing a lot of feature writing for newspapers and magazines. Occasionally – just very occasionally – an interview grew into a friendship. My meeting with the painter Charles Simpson was such a case – not many people today know of his links with Devon. His mother and father lived at Tavistock, in a house near the golf course. It was Charles Simpson who introduced me to the magic of moorland. But for him I would not be writing these words.

'Out on the primitive landscapes of the moors, time suffers a contraction', he once told me. It was Charles too who first made me think about the nature of time. He believed when we come into a stone circle, we come close to the primitive builders of long ago and that, in the very stones, they have left behind something of themselves.

A real all-rounder, he painted a wide range of subjects: land and seascapes, animals and birds. Guy Paget in his book *Sporting Pictures of England* said 'Charles Simpson is undoubtedly the greatest bird painter living. He alone of all artists past and present can make birds appear out of their backgrounds as one approaches them or the light is increased as in nature.'

HERE is an excellent example of Charles Simpson's art: equestrian elegance and movement in a beautiful landscape.

A brilliant painter of horses, he explained to me '… the figure painter finds it difficult to think quadropedially … the born animal painter understands the action of animals *from the first.*'

Like his friend Sir Alfred Munnings, he painted his horses in the traditional representative style, his painterly talents capturing the animal's movement and power. I like to think he would have approved of my active membership of the International League for the Protection of Horses, and I retain a link with the great man through friendship with his daughter Leonora who lives in West Cornwall. We must not forget his portraiture: old and young, men, women and children, he pinned them all to canvas in lifelike detail. At the time I first met Charles, I had just discovered the novels of Crosbie Garstin; he showed me a portrait of the novelist he had done years before. Standing before it, I felt I was meeting Crosbie Garstin.

ONE of my favourite Dartmoor characters, Bowerman's Nose: an old picture postcard.

Beauty is rarely comforting. Beauty can be cruel. As you look at the bones of granite sticking through the soil of Dartmoor you begin to feel the relentless quality of the landscape, an impression intensified when the horizon rolls away like a stretch of sea.

We have a portrait, the eyes of which follow us around the room. Wherever we stand the doctor is looking at you. Brent Tor on the edge of the moor looks at you in the same curious fashion.

There are few more impressive landmarks in all Devon and Cornwall than this tor, crowned by the tiny church, dedicated to St Michael. Thirty seven feet long and but fourteen feet and six inches in width, it is the fourth smallest church in the land. Only the athletic worship or visit here. There is no road for cars. Brides have to walk every inch of the steep slope – it stands 1008 feet above sea level. Not for nothing did Arthur Mee ask: 'Is there anywhere in England a church more romantically poised?'

In his *Book of Dartmoor*, published at the turn of the century, Sabine Baring-Gould recalled how the path to the summit grew:

'*A late curate of Tavistock who took services at Brent Tor and found it often desperate work to scramble to the summit in storm and sleet and rain*

40

BRENT Tor Church on the edge of the moor: A prominent landmark for many miles.

resolved on forming a roadway. He experienced some difficulty in per-
suading men to go out from Tavistock, so he supplied himself with several
bottles of whisky and when he saw a sturdy labourer standing idle in the
marketplace he invited him into his lodgings and plied him with hot grog
until the man in a moist and smiling condition assented to the proposition
that he should give a day to the Brent Tor path.'

Sabine Baring-Gould was a man who wore different talented hats. Squire and parson, author of books, one hundred and fifty of them, hymns including *Onward Christian Soldiers*, he loved Dartmoor and could speak several languages. Builder and landlord, antiquarian and story teller, he packed a lot into his ninety years. He lived in a magical place: Lew Trenchard, now a fine hotel on the edge of the moor; and though he died in 1924 you cannot come to the house or his nearby church and not be aware of his presence. His life reads like something from a novel. He married a Yorkshire mill girl, paid for her education and they raised a large family. One of his ancestors, Madam Margaret Gould, has been *seen* on a number of occasions, for the first time only an hour after she died.

As a member of the Ghost Club Society, I have a rather special interest in Dartmoor's 'other population'.

The ghosts are varied and numerous. One of the most celebrated phantom characters is that of old David Davies, a prisoner who first went to Dartmoor Prison at Princetown in 1879. He spent fifty years at the prison, spending much of that time looking after the sheep. David became known as the Dartmoor shepherd, and when the time of his release came, he asked permission to remain. The request was refused, by the then Home Secretary Winston Churchill. He died in 1929 but his ghostly form has been seen in and around the prison. He was so trusted he was allowed to spend nights on the moor tending expectant ewes: a real Dartmoor character in life and death.

At Cator Common a rare apparition has been sighted – a white dog – and at Gidleigh the sounds of a bloody fight have been heard. I have heard and read accounts of phantom cottages appearing and disappearing, and on visits to Hound Tor I've had the distinct impression of being watched by an invisible somebody. Moreover my lovely collie Rex tended to move cautiously, carefully, in the vicinity of the tor as if he were conscious of an unseen presence.

Phantom hoof beats, black dogs, ghostly music, hairy hands struggling to take control of motor cars: Dartmoor's manifestations cover a wide range of paranormal activity.

If we dismiss half of them as hallucinations, tricks of light – whatever the reason – the remaining fifty percent represent a solid body of evidence. I have a hunch the next century will produce scientific proof confirming the reality of psychic phenomena, and some of those new frontier facts may well occur on the moor. Joan Amos, who lives at Peter Tavy, is a collector of UFO information, and her researches into the subject show there has been much activity in these wide skies.

After thirty years of investigating the supernatural I am of the opinion the majority of manifestations take place in locations either ancient or strong in atmosphere and, of course, here on Dartmoor we have both.

The contrasting qualities of the landscape – ranging from high windswept, sunbleached or sodden in the heart of the moor, beautiful but inhospitable, to farmland on the edges – have made Dartmoor a magnet and a challenge for painters.

The man generally rated 'the one true Dartmoor artist' is Frederick John Widgery who developed a style all of his own, using gouache which has been imitated (unsuccessfully) by many other painters. Gouache is water colour painting in which opaque pigments diluted with water and gum are employed. He also painted in oils using thick colour, something he learnt from his father. Frederick John Widgery died in 1942 but lives on in many fine moorland paintings. Apart from his technical qualities as a painter, Widgery had perception and a rare understanding of Dartmoor. His gift for combining colour and form captured the subtleties and the very spirit of the terrain.

And what terrain. This is not only an ancient landscape, the sheer loneliness of parts of the moor get hold of you and, above all, you discover and rediscover the best way to recapture the spirit of times past is to get off the well worn paths and tracks and venture into this secret wilderness.

THE lovely thatched pavilion at Instow.

NICHOLAS GEORGE, a remarkable first century for the Crusaders.

CRICKET AT INSTOW and THE VALLEY OF ROCKS

IDOUBT if there be any scene in the world more animating or delightful than a cricket match!... That was said by Mary Russell Mitford and, of course, she is correct.

Cricket grounds establish a tradition and an individuality of their own. They have an impact, sometimes subtle, whether we are players or spectators. Two of my favourite grounds are high on the coast of North Devon.

If I were brought blindfolded to Instow, where the North Devon Club plays its cricket, I should know immediately, instinctively that I was *here*. There is something in the air – and the turf.

The real joy of this ground is the thatched pavilion – a rare and glorious sight – it was originally a barn, old even when the cricketers first pitched stumps at Instow as long ago as 1832.

There is an open beauty here, but when the winds blow – and they can really blow along this northern coastline – there can be problems of communication between the captain and his fielders, especially those in the deep. I know from personal experience, for when I captained a touring team at Instow in the 1950s the wind was so strong we played the match without bails! For me it was a memorable Saturday morning, taking three catches in quite quick succession before lunch: the result of some very fine bowling with the new ball by Maurice Weeks of Penzance who went on to play cricket and football for Cornwall. Maurice's accurate thoughtful bowling forced the batsmen into all sorts of errors, sending three relatively simple chances to forward short leg. We still lost the match: our only defeat of the week.

Nevertheless Instow, despite that disappointing result, made a tremendous impression. More than thirty years later, I came back with the Cornish Crusaders, no longer a player, now club president and occasionally scorer in the scorebox, and still the magic worked. I suppose first impressions are difficult to put aside. Colours and qualities of light and atmosphere may change in a changing season, but there is an eternal something about this Instow ground.

Herein lies much of cricket's charm and appeal. In an uprooted world, the game has strong roots. That wise and witty cricket writer Denzil Batchelor once reflected: 'When I watch it for an hour, or a day, or a season, I am catching a glimpse, a halcyon flash, of a great pageant which stretches far back into our history … ' And I get that sense of awe and continuity here at Instow.

As a loyal member of Gloucestershire County Cricket Club, I take pride in the fact David Shepherd, one of cricket's splendid characters, hails from this neck of the Devonshire woods. Today one of the most respected umpires in the world, David made a dozen centuries for Gloucestershire. He struck the ball mighty blows, but they were often handsome strokes. With his generous waistline, it is difficult to picture him as a scrum half on the Rugby field, but reliable folk in North Devon tell me he was precisely that in his younger days. First, as a cricketer and later as an umpire, he has caused and continued to cause immense amusement with his antics whenever the score is 111.

Many cricketers detest the 'Lord Nelson'. This cricketing curse is when the scoreboard reads 111 – the three ones. It is an odd and curious fact that many batsmen do get out when the scoreboard shows that seemingly ominous number. The expression 'Lord Nelson' is due to the fact the famous Admiral had one eye, one arm and 'one unmentionable piece of anatomy'.

To move from Instow to the Valley of Rocks is to move from one lovely cricket ground to another. The Lynton and Lynmouth club is fortunate to play in surely one of the most beautiful and dramatic settings in the whole of the Westcountry. They have been playing cricket here since 1876.

Over the years the game has grown deeply into the English countryside – our cricket ground fits naturally and historically into the landscape like the village inn or the church. But you simply do not expect to find a cricket ground in the Valley of Rocks, just one mile from Lynmouth.

The poet Southey came here and was conquered by the impressive amphitheatre: *'Imagine a narrow vale between two ridges of hills, somewhat steep; the southern hill turfed; the vale, which runs from east to west, covered with huge stones and fragments of stone among the fern that fills it; the northern ridge completely bare, excoriated of all turf and all soil, the very bones and skeletons of the earth; rock reeling upon rock, stone piled upon stone, a huge terrific mass. I ascended, with some toil, the highest point; two large stones inclining on each other formed a rude portal on the summit.'*

In a certain light, near dusk, you could swear the Valley is peopled by men and women and not just rocks. Maybe that isn't such a fanciful idea either, because according to legend they were once humans, turned to stone for some frivolous behaviour, like dancing or hurling on a Sunday.

I was last here on the cricket ground in August 1992, when there was a batting blitz from young Nicholas George of St Buryan. Coming in first wicket down for the Cornish Crusaders, Nicholas batted like a modern Gilbert Jessop: his first century, 114 to be precise, coming in just thirty-three scoring strokes – eleven sixes and seven boundaries. This was no mere left-handed slogging but an innings dominated by a fine sense of timing and the power of his driving, the ball flying in all directions, giving the illusion that somehow this small ground had suddenly shrunk in size.

I have, too, one lovely cricketing story concerning the Valley of Rocks. Grahame Parker, the former Gloucestershire batsman, Cambridge University Captain and England Rugby full-back, told me he played here as a young man on a club tour. Fielding in the covers, he found his boots soon coated in a curious kind of lime. During the interval, Grahame politely enquired about the lime in the covers. 'Oh, no,' said the groundsman, 'that's not lime. Our club secretary died last week, and his ashes were scattered over there this morning.'

*　　*　　*　　*　　*

EXMOOR

WE must not forget an important geographical fact: parts of Exmoor belong to Devon. Here in the Westcountry we are proud of our moors, all have their qualities and different admirers, but most fairminded people would say 'Exmoor is the most beautiful'. The truth is, Exmoor is unique. Exmoor is the essence of the countryside without that barren abandoned air which hangs over so many moorland areas. Here the landscape is broken by undulating valleys threaded by streams which are almost too pretty to be true. In autumn it has rich colour and beauty, and anytime in the calendar it has some of the finest riding country in Britain. More than a quarter of a century ago I rode on Exmoor: treasured vivid memories.

Exmoor, like the moors of Penwith, have an advantage over Dartmoor and Bodmin Moor; they run along the coast within sight and sometimes sound of the sea. In both cases the seascape enhances the moor. On Exmoor on a diamond-sharp day you can see Wales.

In 1989 I commissioned Polly Lloyd to do a book on Exmoor for Bossiney. After an early visit to Exmoor, she wrote to me saying 'I'm not only delighted to be doing another book for you but I'm delighted to be discovering Exmoor and I aim to keep on rediscovering it ... for all lovers of the English countryside, it is a cameo to be treasured ... '

Polly Lloyd, a well-known voice on regional radio and news reader for television from Bristol, not only enjoyed the project, she produced a valuable addition to the Bossiney list. A literary gent congratulated me, 'Polly is a good choice,' he said, 'she's brought the

A RIDER surveys the scene on Brendon Common.

freshness of an outsider to the Exmoor scene.'

On the very opening page of *About Exmoor*, she wrote:

'Once discovered, Exmoor can never be ignored. It seems to change character with every twist of the road, one moment bleak, magnificent moor, the next green valley dotted with farms. Its villages are timeless but never outdated, its coastline in turn majestic and gentle – and cruel. In a way it is a turbulent part of the country, as if someone has taken the patchwork of fields and lanes and given it a good shake, letting it fall in a rumpled fashion. And perhaps because of its unpredictability, man over the years has had to fit in to suit the land, never quite taming it completely.'

As publishers we have produced four Exmoor titles, and the area has been featured in several others. You soon discover there are layers and layers of Exmoor experience. You realize too only the foolish would be dogmatic about the place: what it has to offer must be received individually and with a degree of humility. But this much I do know: the landscape never beckons you on with unfulfilled promise. There is a spiritual intimacy between the traveller and this countryside, especially true when you are on horse-

49

back. The ghosts on Exmoor are surely gentle ghosts, characters reluctant to leave – and who can blame them?

I have known Exmoor in all four seasons, but am unsure whether spring or autumn are its best times. May is the month for optimism when Devon's gardens cry out with colour, an anticipation not easily defined. The wild flowers of the county too, make it one of the richest in all England: a kind of Fort Knox. Autumn has its charms – there are often lovely days in October. Not for nothing do country folk call it 'St Luke's Little Summer.' Then the shades of the trees and the bracken on the moor have a special something, but the days are shortening. Sonia has driven me across Exmoor when snow flakes have been fluttering from a dark sky, and we still rated it a magical landscape.

Comparisons with Dartmoor are inevitable – and futile. Dartmoor reminds you of ancient history. Exmoor does not. Dartmoor has a strong sense of desolation. There is no such aura here. Exmoor is minus those outcrops of granite. Here the land is well covered and the lanes bordered by hedges. Arthur Mee usually got it right, and when he came to Exmoor more than fifty years ago, he wrote in his notebook: ' … incomparable glory of nature on the heights and in the hollows.'

James Turner was a gifted writer about the landscape – I am writing these words at a desk which once belonged to him so in a sense he is never far away. Bossiney was soon to launch its first Exmoor title, we were having an early evening drink, and I asked him how he rated Exmoor – truth is we both responded to moorland in our different ways. He was currently working on a big book about the countryside of Britain for London publishers which was published after his death. He thought for a few moments and then said: 'Exmoor is more intimate, gentler and more beautiful than any other moorland I've met.'

That sentence probably says it all.

* * * * *

SARAH FOOT lives in a beautiful converted barn at Elmgate, overlooking the River Lynher, and she has strong family links with Cornwall. Her grandfather Isaac Foot was Lord Mayor of Plymouth, and her father Hugh Caradon was born in the city. She lived for some years by the Tamar, and knows and loves both western and eastern banks of the great river.

Before becoming involved with full time social work, first at Derriford Hospital and now at St Luke's Hospice in Plymouth, Sarah Foot was a prolific contributor to the Bossiney list. She made several television appearances and many radio broadcasts.

In 1994 Sarah Foot introduced **Secret Devon**, *in which six writers made six journeys.*

SARAH FOOT, photographed in 1976, with Trematon Castle Gatehouse ▶ *in the background.*

51

PENWITH

D RIVE down fron the flinty town of St Just-in-Penwith – so different from the St Just-in-Roseland – and follow the winding land of high stone walls and you come to that most magical of Cornish Coves – Cape Cornwall.

This was once thought to be the most westerly point of Cornwall and was documented as such in Spenser's account of journeying home from Ireland with Walter Raleigh in 1589. To the right as you descend the steep lane are a stone wall and small fields like a chequer board leading to a rising lump of land before it falls dramatically to the sea. Beyond lie the two rocks, The Brisons, that have proved such a danger to fisher folk and sailors of all vessels circumnavigating this rocky area. Many a ship has been wrecked there.

It was a lucky day when the National Trust acquired this stretch of unspoilt land to protect it from developers. The mixture of green fields, high hedges and stone walls with the sea beyond, sometimes angry grey or other times a brilliant almost navy blue, makes this a particularly breathtaking visit. There are few better places to see the wilderness that makes this stretch of Cornish coastline so powerfully beautiful.

I am convinced that the most dramatic drive in the world is from St Just to St Ives. The winding treacherous road runs some ten miles along the coast on one side and the barren rocky moor on the other.

All the best and most haunting of Cornwall lies there. This was the real harsh mining country. Botallack Mine with its gaunt but splendid mine house right down on the cliffs may seem beautiful and romantic now but it is well to remember the hardship of the men who worked there; they worked away several fathoms below the sea. Many of them never saw daylight for months at a time. Pendeen, Levant, Geevor, all these mines lie along that driveway.

Up above, on the moorland side of the road, lie huge granite mounds and in amongst that land are remains of Bronze Age and Iron Age settlements, old standing stones and tombs and fogous. You feel this is a land without time, that however much things change those ancient monuments hold their own. Those mine house relics remind us too of all that made Cornwall work. Whether the years before Christ or just a hundred years ago, the past does not leave this Cornish landscape easily – it stays, brooding, ever present to become part of its land, its atmosphere, its people. You are never in England when you are in Cornwall, there is something so intrinsically different and this is especially so in West Penwith.

Driving back to the Devon borders after a visit to those western ends of Cornwall you feel as if you have been abroad where a totally different culture, landscape and people exist. John Heath-Stubb's resounding poem recalls the essence of this landscape:

'This is a hideous and wicked country,
Sloping to hateful sunsets and the end of time,
Hollow with mine shafts, naked with granite, fanatic
With sorrow, abortions of the past
Hop through these bogs; black faced, the villagers
Remember burnings by the hewn stones'.

You carry with you not only that breathtaking scenery from Cape Cornwall and the rugged moorland and stark mine houses but also the legends that have lived in those areas. No legend can be quite so haunting as that of the Mermaid of Zennor whose figure was carved into a fifteenth century bench-end for Zennor church lest we forget. She was the mermaid who haunted a young man from the choir of Zennor Church and eventually seduced him into joining her in a world beneath the sea. She wooed him with her beautiful voice. And that is another thing that Cornish people reckon is worth respecting – music. However hard the life of fishermen, farmers and miners might be they have always respected musicians and artists and writers. Perhaps this is why so many artists are drawn to Cornwall.

In the centre of St Just is the Plain-an-Gwarry, an amphitheatre where Cornish miracle plays were once acted and later in the eighteenth century Cornish wrestling bouts took place. It was in this fine setting Dr A L Rowse, the Cornish historian, writer and poet, and Dame Barbara Hepworth, the sculptor, were given the honour of being made Cornish Bards.

Artists and writers have always been honoured in Cornwall and it is a fine thing that the new Tate Gallery at St Ives houses the works of the modern artists of St Ives and thereabouts – Patrick Heron whose house lies on that road between Cape Cornwall and St Ives is only one of the living artists whose work is on show there. Potters, artists, sculptors, painters, writers and poets who have worked in Cornwall, whether they are Cornish or not, are always influenced by the past and present of Cornwall and by its scenery, whether the rugged west or north coast or the gentler river valleys. Maybe Cornwall's most distinctive feature is its failure to be pretentious – the countryside and its people are inclined to demand to be accepted as they are and if you cannot accept their directness that is your loss, not theirs.

PENWITH coast near St Just.

BODMIN MOOR

THE VERY words conjure up a myriad of images and emotions first conjured up for me by my grandfather and father and then by many other people throughout my life.

I can see and hear now, my grandfather sitting back in his easy chair in the library of his Cornish home, pipe in hand, book on his knee, discussing some walk he had enjoyed in his early married years when he had taken his family to live at St Cleer at the foot of Caradon Hill. Brown Willy, Rough Tor, Caradon, St Breward, Bolventor were names that rolled off my grandfather's Westcountry tongue like musical notes. In those St Cleer days he would wake early and walk across the moor to Liskeard to catch a train to Plymouth and his solicitor's practice there.

Most people would find this an exciting walk perhaps once or twice a year and in mild temperate weather, few would have the enthusiasm to love it as much as he did seeking out new pleasures on each foray. My grandmother would take the donkey and the jingle to meet him in the evening and I often try to reconstruct the picture of them returning home in evening light to that little house on the moor bulging with seven children. All his five sons became great walkers and explorers of the moor. From their early youth they were walking up Brown Willy and Rough Tor. No wonder the wide moulded vistas of hillocks, rocks, streams and gorse and heather became part of their very souls.

ISAAC Foot, a Westcountry crusader, a radical Liberal, staunch ▶ *Methodist, orator and lawyer, a lover of Life, a learned man who taught himself everything he knew – and the father of the most celebrated family in the west.*

My father, always as intrigued by people as places, found where a gypsy encampment was not far from their house. Eagerly and nervously he begged to join their group and was delighted to be accepted into their gathering. Listening to their talk, watching their work, taking in their habits and their ways was only the beginning of a fascination with people of different cultures. It was not that many years later that he was learning to get on with Arab communities in Palestine where he first started his career as a Colonial Servant and all through his life he was meeting and being intrigued by Cypriots, Africans, West Indians; never losing his desire to be accepted and to understand people who were different from him. But this great enthusiasm of his life started with the gypsies of Bodmin Moor.

Just as I can hear, ringing in my memory, my grandfather's rich brogue reciting those names of Brown Willy, Rough Tor, Bolventor so I can remember another great lover of Bodmin Moor, Joe Halls. Last week I drove up to Bodmin Moor on the new A30 dual carriageway that cuts and scars the moor but cannot destroy it, I turned off at Jamaica Inn and took that windy road that I believe is one of the prettiest drives in the world. It goes from Bolventor down to Golitha Falls following the early Fowey River all the way. You pass the driveway to Carkeet and Joe Halls' house that way. Joe died some ten years ago but his voice and character will stay forever in my head and in my heart. Meeting him and knowing him was one of the great bonuses in my life. If my grandfather first opened my mind and senses to the mysteries of Bodmin Moor, Joe Halls revived them and gave me new images to dwell on.

Joe Halls started his life as a farm hand and ended it owning over a thousand acres of the moor. There was nothing cosy or tranquil about Joe Halls' feelings for Bodmin Moor. This was a land of hard graft – something to be tackled and fought and a land that could overcome you, defeat you, or harden you to all gentleness. He had lived in the granite house on the edge of the moor without comforts or distractions. No electricity, no motor cars or television. Fires were lit with peat dug from the moor, cattle were rounded up by horse and the only outside entertainment were services – twice on Sundays – at the little chapel at Bolventor.

One of the lasting images Joe Halls gave me of Bodmin Moor

was the sight he remembered on winter evenings when people from all over the moor converged on the chapel carrying lanterns in their hands so that the whole landscape was dotted with little dancing lights like fireflies or glow-worms homing on a great magnet. Methodism was that great magnet that drew men and women to worship. Joe ended his life in pain from the chilblains and rheumatism that had set in. His wife left the house on the moor, unable to bear the harshness anymore. Joe literally had to be carried out to live his last months in greater comfort in a village bungalow. But he went on pining and as he would say 'regretting and deploring' the challenge of moor life. I once was stupid enough to ask him whether he loved the moor. 'Love it?' he asked eyebrows raised and pushing back the little woollen hat he always wore indoors or out. 'No I don't love it, just can't live without it'.

No-one who has fallen under the spell of the moor can disregard how Daphne du Maurier wrote about it. As a young woman she first felt and began to understand the harsh reality of the place.

When I was writing a book about the River Fowey I met Sir Arthur Quiller Couch's daughter Foy. She told me the story of how Daphne had asked her to come and explore the moor. They had stayed at Jamaica Inn and then set out on ponies to discover as much of the moor as they could. It had been a bright sunny morning when they set out. Inexperienced as they were, they had not realised the quick changing face of the moor. Before long a heavy mist had fallen and the two young women were totally lost. In the ensuing hours they tried to find their way home, eventually it was the moorland ponies who detected their route back to safety and they began to understand the real trickery and the mystery of those barren acres of land. Some of this was later transcribed in Dame Daphne's novel *Jamaica Inn*.

When my children were small I took them to Bodmin Moor to sit on those great slabs of rock at Cheesewring and to walk across to the Hurlers by St Cleer. They had seen Caradon Hill long before there was a television mast and they've understood a little bit why their grandfather took his name from these parts when he became a life peer and called himself Lord Caradon of St Cleer. This will be our family inheritance. Not possessions or habitations but a passing down through the family line of a respect and a need to try and understand that compelling force that draws us to the moor, yet rejects all false emotions calling only for a baring of our true selves.

It is not surprising that cruel and terrible things happen on the moor and this was something that Daphne du Maurier captured so well in *Jamaica Inn*. But what is so beguiling about the moor is that it can enchant with its great beauty as much as its harshness and severity.

One midsummer day not long ago I walked with a friend to Brown Willy and Rough Tor. The blueness of the arch of sky above contrasted with rolling white clouds moving shadows on the bracken and rocks below. Dragonflies skimmed the river, buzzards mewed above, otherwise the silence was complete the beauty all around quite literally breathtaking. We sat on the rocks and marvelled at it all. Summer or winter this was a place to hold part of us forever. As E C Axford put it, Bodmin Moor is a 'wilderness in miniature, full of contrasts; whatever the weather, the sense of loneliness and antiquity is persistent'.

Although the main A30 has burgeoned into a main dual carriageway carving straight through the centre of the moor it cannot defile the atmosphere. Just a mile or less away from the busy traffic you can escape into a new dimension, into solitude and wilderness.

KIT HILL above Callington – a prominent Cornish landmark.

CALLINGTON

I T WAS October 1939 – I was six weeks old – the month after the Second World War was declared and my mother brought me to Callington, to my grandfather's house Pencrebar.

From that time forward it remained my home base throughout my childhood. It is the place where so much of my childhood nostalgia is rooted. Some people feel Callington is an uninteresting town, but then they did not have the pleasure of growing up there, enjoying childhood holidays in the near vicinity and having a family there. My great great grandfather Mr William Dingle – otherwise known as Gruffy, was a Callington man. In 1846 he married a woman called Arabella and together they became pillars of the middle class, trading community of the nineteenth century.

Devout Methodists, they gave money for the chapel, donated a manse for the Minister and bought and renovated a storage building (once a mine engine house) known as Kit Hill Castle into a kind of convalescent home or the equivalent of today's health farm. In *Venning's Directory* of 1901 he described it as 'a health resort', and goes on to say:

'The place is becoming every year increasingly popular, and visitors after staying there for a short time, have been greatly invigorated and improved in health by the bracing and salubrious air of Kit Hill and greatly enchanted by the scenery – this place has been greatly recommended for invalids by some eminent physicians and doctors, a few of whom have been there to stay themselves'.

Knowing and loving Kit Hill as I do I find it hard to believe that the air was ever 'bracing and salubrious' – if ever there is likely to be mist or fog in the region it is bound to be around Kit Hill. However, there was at that time a great call for these 'health

PENCREBAR at Callington, Isaac Foot's much loved home. 'I have loved the habitation of thy house: and the place whence thine honour dwelleth.' PSALM XXII Verse 8.

resorts' for people living under the increasing smog and unhealthy atmosphere of the cities created by the Industrial Revolution.

Kit Hill has one of the most panoramic views in all of Cornwall and it has an historic background – numerous earth works, remains of trenches and encampments of Roman origin are still to be found there and pieces of battle axes, flint implements and other weapons of war have been discovered. Kit Hill also had a famous granite quarry in the nineteenth and early twentieth century with about a hundred men being employed in the Kit Hill Granite Quarries. This granite was used in construction of the Thames Embankment, Blackfriars Bridge, the fortifications around Plymouth, and Battersea Bridge in London. Now the quarry remains a scar in the hill – somehow full of melancholy with its deep basin of water below.

Gruffy and Arabella Dingle had a daughter called Sarah. When I was born my grandfather Isaac Foot – who married Gruffy and

Arabella's granddaughter Eva – christened me Sarah Dingle after his mother-in-law. I was christened in the chapel at Callington, in the school room where my grandmother had taught Sunday School.

My grandmother had lived with her grandparents in Callington and had met my grandfather through their Methodist connections. When they were married they went to live in Plymouth, then at St Cleer on Bodmin Moor, and finally at Pencrebar at Callington. It had always been my grandmother's most fervent wish that they should return to Callington. My grandfather easily succumbed, eventually becoming a committed Callington man.

Now it may seem an uninspiring town to those who pass through but just looking at its historical background conjures up great images – this summary of Callington's history and leading events comes from *Venning's Directory 1901:*

V Century

King Arthur kept his palace and court in the early part of the century at Callington, then called Killiwick. Hingston Down is supposed to be the scene of some of his battles.

IX Century

Battle on Hingston Down (just by Kit Hill) between Saxons and Danes the latter defeated by Egbert.

XI Century

KIT HILL, a Foot family favourite and an outstanding landmark for many miles.

Callington in Domesday Book called Calweton. This manor belonged to the Duke of Cornwall and King of Britain.

XII & XIII Centuries

The Parliament of Tinners for Devon and Cornwall assembled at Kit Hill every 7th or 8th year for conference.

XIII Century

Henry III granted Market Charter for the town.

XV Century

New bridge on the Lynher built – church built.

Enough to raise anyone's interest and Callington people are very proud of their past.

Ten years ago David Young, architect and media man, asked me to accompany him for one of his television programmes. 'Choose any town in Cornwall or Devon to visit' he said. I answered without hesitation 'Callington'. He was somewhat bemused. 'Is there anything of architectural interest there?' he said. But in fact it is not only the historical past, or the architectural interests that draw me to Callington. It is the fact that when I walk down the Fore Street I remember my childhood, going to the saddler to buy pieces of tack for my aunt's ponies and smelling the leather. It is the memory of driving to chapel with my grandfather on Sunday mornings and listening to the rousing sermons.

It was 1787 when it is reputed that the first methodist preacher came to Callington and 1845 the Wesleyan Chapel was built. As far as we were concerned as children, Callington people were mostly Methodists and mostly Liberals – I know that this was not entirely true but I never even entered the beautiful church of St Mary until I was grown up and married.

From Callington we came to know Kit Hill, the Lynher River, the views of Bodmin Moor and the comforting feeling of belonging to a community that cared about its own people. Now, fifty-five years after I first went to Callington as an infant I can still walk down the Fore Street and feel that sense of belonging.

SIR HUGH FOOT, later Lord Caradon, with Princess Margaret in 1955. He loved the Caradon area of Bodmin Moor, and represented Britain at the United Nations. ▶

HOUSES I HAVE
LOVED IN CORNWALL

THE first Cornish house I ever loved was my grandfather's house near Callington. Pencrebar was home to our family all through my childhood and because my parents lived abroad when I was young it became our home base. It was a house of perfect magic for me containing everything a child could possibly dream about.

Firstly, it was headed by a magnanimous and cheerful grandfather, who, despite being teetotal and nonconformist, was convinced life was for enjoying and very soon persuaded his grandchildren this was of prime importance.

Pencrebar is a large Victorian house with seven bedrooms, large reception rooms and endless kitchens, pantries and laundry rooms. It was base for my six loving and fascinating uncles and aunts and for my parents when they were in England. It also housed my grandfather's huge library, believed to be the largest privately collected in the country, and it was always full of music. My grandfather played his grand piano with more gusto than expertise and thumped out the chords of his favourite hymns whilst singing out the words with great enthusiasm. When he was not playing the piano his radiogram would be playing at full volume filling the house with Bach, Beethoven and Mendelsohn.

At the top of the house there were five attic rooms used by my uncles for their studies and they had a wonderfully musty and cobwebby feel to them. The views from these studies down the Lynher valley were quite beautiful and remain clearly in my mind to this day. The stairs were covered in piles of books and to get into the lavatories required climbing over stacks of yet more books.

PLACE, home of the Treffrys since the 1300s. It is one of the great houses of Cornwall. Wherever you go in and around Fowey, Place seems to watch you.

The bedrooms were named after the principal books housed in them – the Milton room, the Old Testament Room, the Cromwell Room. In the library room itself my grandfather spent his later years reading and yet he never minded our comings and goings, looking up with a cheerful smile or tapping us playfully on the head as we sat playing at his knee.

One of my aunts lived for animals so that there were always a number of dogs, usually Irish Setters, though she later showed a preference for Pekinese. In the stables ponies and horses were lovingly cared for and the old tennis court was turned into a school for them. My aunt ran a riding school for local people and her students included adults and children of every shape, size and background. The result was that there was never a moment without something wonderful to do – if we were not with the horses and dogs we were playing down by the River Lynher, walking for miles in the fields and through the bluebell woods or playing rowdy games with our uncles on the lawn. In the evenings we listened to *Children's Hour* by the open fire in the library whilst we munched through slabs of

LADY CARADON at Trematon Castle.

fresh crispy white bread spread with Marmite. On Sundays it was scones and cream or saffron cake and high tea was often perfected with junket and cream. No house could ever live up to the magical atmosphere of Pencrebar.

When Pencrebar was sold, after the death of my grandfather, I felt as if I had lost something that could never be regained but very soon after my parents took the tenancy of Trematon Castle, a grand house built within the old castle walls and which belonged to the Duchy of Cornwall since the first Duke of Cornwall, the Black Prince, and is situated above the estuary of the River Lynher. The building of the castle was begun in 1080 by Robert of Mortain with great walls surrounding a keep which tops a man-made mound.

Nowadays the banks of the keep are a sight to behold particularly in the spring when daffodils, primroses and bluebells grow in profusion. In the keep itself the holes for the old beams are still to be seen, one of which for many years has been the home for a pair of sparrowhawks. The gatehouse has two large rooms on separate floors with great granite fireplaces in both. It is here that the Black Prince is said to have stayed when he visited the castle. Trematon was to my children what Pencrebar was to me and these two ancient buildings, the Keep and the gatehouse, became their and their cousins' playground. They loved the legend that Sir Francis Drake had stored his treasure somewhere in the grounds of Trematon after he had singed the King of Spain's beard. They lived in hope that one day they would find this historic hoard. There is a cave at the foot of the Keep where they were certain that the treasure must be.

The house itself, simple and rectangular, was built by Benjamin Tucker in 1807 and was painted in the palest pink when my parents lived there. Tucker pulled down part of the curtain wall, something that would be thought totally unacceptable today, but which created wonderful views from the house down to the River Lynher and on to Devonport and Plymouth beyond and across the river to the wooded slopes of another stately Cornish house, Antony.

When my parents moved to Trematon Castle in 1962 the gardens had become somewhat neglected. With great enthusiasm and energy my mother set about retrieving from the undergrowth those parts of the garden which were nearly lost – so the orchard beyond the

TREMATON: it was Benjamin Tucker who built a house within the castle walls.

gatehouse, the Italian garden and the old wooded carriage way winding down to the village of Forder below were reinstated. She became very excited as she found lost rose gardens, Italian statues and wide brick and granite steps leading from one part of the garden to others. The front of the house overlooking the river led onto a slate terrace and a wide flat lawn – perfect for endless games of croquet – and this in turn led down to more granite steps, and another terrace bordered with tall Queen Elizabeth pink roses and walls of trailing rosemary. All around the lawn were white, russet red, pale pink and blue hydrangeas dominated by a wide and perfect beech tree giving shade to the arduous activities of the croquet players.

The inside of the house was cleverly designed with suites of rooms, all of them with views across to the curtain walls or down to the river. From my parents' bedroom where the windows reached from floor to ceiling you were able to watch the trains making their way either down to Penzance or on into Plymouth. Likewise, if travelling by train you could catch the most wonderful view of Trematon with its Keep and Gatehouse as you crossed the viaduct at Antony passage.

For twenty-five years I took my children two or three times a year for holidays at Trematon – once we lived there for six months when my husband was abroad. It became to us all a paradise of safety and fun. When my mother, who had loved the house and garden so intensely, and who had filled it with family and friends over the twenty years she lived there, died, my son, shattered by her sudden going, clambered up through the woods during the night and sat in the middle of the ancient keep. He sat there for an hour or so in the silent darkness and remembered her. He did not tell of this for many months. I thought it was something she would have greatly appreciated. It was, I think, a fine memorial. She had given so much to my children and their cousins, something that has stayed with them as they have grown up. Something that can never be taken away from them – a place can only be truly magical if it is loved by those who have lived in it.

This is very true of my other two favourite Cornish houses – Port Eliot at St Germans and Place at Fowey. They are both unique houses, they are both intrinsically Cornish and bound up in Cornish history and they are lucky houses as they are lived in by people who love them and appreciate them.

I remember as a child being taken to tea at Port Eliot. The thing

PORT ELIOT at St Germans, one of the stately homes of Cornwall. Photograph by David Hambly LMPA, Windsor Place, Liskeard.

that remains most with me about that occasion is the atmosphere of the house, filled with beautiful things where the furnishings, carpets and curtains seemed to have been there forever. But I also remember, even at the age of eight, being so impressed by the lie of the parkland around the house – it seemed to entice me out into it to run and play in its undulating greenness. The house was passed straight from his grandparents to Peregrine Eliot, now the Earl of St Germans, and because he has never known any other home he is truly part of it and loves and knows every inch.

Lord St Germans says with pride the earliest recording of a habitation at Port Eliot was in the seventh century. When I asked him the most important thing about Port Eliot he says it's to do with its antiquity – that in some way it has always been there. But just as he loves the antiquity he is also courageous enough to have added modern art to the house. In the elegant Round Room he commissioned Robert Lenkiewicz to paint a mural on every inch of the curved walls. The figures depict all the best known characters of today's Cornwall and all those who have been closest to Lord St Germans over the years. It is a staggering and intriguing work of art that could only have been conceived and executed by someone with the courage of their convictions. The Round Room has seen some great occasions including concerts given by the East Cornwall Bach Society and reading of his poems by Sir John Betjeman and it is impressive to see how well the old and the new are able to mix.

This mixture of ancient and modern has become the speciality of the present Lord St German. Perhaps the musical occasions best remembered at Port Eliot were the annual Elephant Fayres. They were great gatherings of people from all walks of life with celebrations of modern and rock music and drama mixed with arts and crafts all of which took place in the grounds of Port Eliot. For this reason he became affectionately known as the 'Hippy Lord', but hippy lord or no, he not only appreciates the antiquity of his abode but also has the perception to recognise many of the finer artists and writers of his age. For many years he has housed these intellectuals and craftsmen in and around Port Eliot, encouraging them in their work and giving them the time, the space, the peace and respect to achieve so much. There is nothing very modern about this as there is a long tradition of Cornish aristocrats becoming patrons to the artists of their day.

The Eliot family has lived in Port Eliot since the Reformation and in the great monastic church which lies beside the house and towers above it are many Eliot tombs and monuments. Perhaps the fact that Port Eliot was built on the site of an old priory is one of the reasons why it retains such a very special atmosphere and, certainly, the importance of the church, which was the cathedral church of Cornwall from 930 to 1040, gives a unique place in the history of Cornwall.

This little poem by A L Rowse referring to my mother at Trematon Castle, Lady St Germans, the grandmother of the present Lord St Germans, at Port Eliot, and Nancy Astor in Plymouth brings back many happy memories for me.

Friends Gone Before

All the people who accompanied me
Through life are vanishing, one by one.
In the train we pass by Trematon,
Lived in by my friends the Caradons
No longer, with Sylvia the spirit gone.
Whither fled? She was the soul of the place,
Grande dame and gardener, hospitable,
Kindly and loving, generous with her plants.
And now St Germans, where Nellie presided at Port
Of the Eliots, and bravely held the Fort,
The friend of Nancy Astor and Bernard Shaw.
Here is Nancy's Plymouth, never the same
Without her on the Hoe, playing her game
To the gallery, her bemused electorate.
Sometimes when in the city I step aside
Into St Andrew's to stand and remember her.
All three are gone, good women in their day,
For whom, alone on my way, I sigh, and pray.

A.L.Rowse

73

Though the mansion of Place at Fowey differs so much from Port Eliot their similarities are what have gained my particular affection. Whilst Port Eliot is essentially rural and the centre of a large estate and the village of St Germans, relying on its parkland and river setting for its particular magic, Place, on the other hand, is a stately house within a town. A L Rowse, in his book *The Little Land of Cornwall* writes: *'The fascinating and historic town of Fowey is entirely dominated by the no less historic and fascinating mansion of Place to a degree rarely paralleled.'*

To drive down through the gates of Place, turning off one of the narrow streets of Fowey, is an extraordinary experience. The wide drive curves down steeply towards the river, until you feel you might drive right into the estuary. The house with its granite carvings reaches up above with its high tower and beyond, the grand estuary is festooned with vessels of every sort: tugs, yachts, the lifeboat, dredgers, dinghies and, on occasions magnificently enough, tall ships and warships are anchored there. Now and then merchant vessels, from all over the world, can be seen working their way up the estuary to collect their cargoes of china clay. The sight is reminiscent of a child's story book illustration, so full of colour, variety and activity.

The first time I visited Place was when Mrs Anne Treffry was living there alone. With great kindness she showed me around the handsome house. As I climbed up the circular stone steps to the front door I sensed I was entering a fortress and the house has, indeed, been fortified over the centuries by the Treffry family fending off the Dutch, Spanish and French invaders of the port of Fowey. You feel the same sense of antiquity in this house as you do at Port Eliot. In the Porphyry Hall or the library panelled in wood from the timbers of the frigate Bellerophon, the vessel which took Napoleon into exile after the Hundred Days War, and the drawing room with its intricate plaster ceiling, its antique furniture and carpets, curtains and wallpaper, there is nothing new about Place. Maybe, as with Port Eliot, the fact that the house was built on the site of a priory, in this case Tywardreath, it has its own special atmosphere. I am also sure that the same family living in the house since it was built adds a sense of endurance, and both Port Eliot and Place are still lived in and enjoyed by the same families. How long this will continue is hard to say today, as with all large family houses there is the continual struggle to maintain and keep them as near as possible to how they have always been. We may now be witnessing the end of a way of life that has gone on for many centuries. Many of the great houses of Cornwall are now cared for by the National Trust and for this we must all be grateful. It is a marvellous fact that so many people are interested in their heritage and visit the Trust's many houses in such great numbers, but it remains true that the atmosphere of a house is changed once it is opened to the public. A part of our way of life, whether for better or worse, will be gone forever, when there are no more houses left such as Place and Port Eliot.

David Treffry, recently High Sheriff of Cornwall, who previously worked with the International Monetary Fund in Washington now lives at Place. With great application he has recovered much of the gardens originally reorganised and planned by T H Mawson in 1900. He fills the house with people from all walks of life and, in particular those who contribute towards life in Cornwall in any way. As a result the house is now enjoyed by both the young and the old of Cornwall as well as many visitors from all over the world.

John Leland, Henry VIII's antiquarian and chaplain, commented in 1538 that Thomas Treffry *'builded a righte fair and stronge embeteled tower in his house and embatteling all the walls of the house in a manner made it a castelle'*. It is this tower that can be seen from almost any vantage point in the narrow streets of Fowey. Later, in the 19th-century, Joseph Thomas Austen inherited the house through his mother and later, when he was High Sheriff, took the name of Treffry and rebuilt it in a Regency Gothic style. Joseph Thomas was a remarkable industrialist and amongst his other accomplishments was responsible for the building of the Treffry viaduct set in the beautiful Luxulyan valley, now owned, for posterity, by the Cornwall Heritage Trust.

It was this magnate who not only added so much to Place in the way of granite towers and the Porphyry Hall but was also responsible for the remarkable carvings both inside and outside the house. Most interesting, from my point of view, are the carvings by the Cornish sculptor Neville Northey Burnard, from Altarnun. His first commission was to work on the new additions to Place and this was only the beginning of a notable career. He subsequently won the Silver Medal of the Royal Cornwall Polytechnic Society, a body especially formed to encourage local artists, and then went to London to apply his skills under commissions from many rich and famous people including a bust of the Prince of Wales (later Edward VII). He later became a sad drunk ending his remarkable career wandering from house to house in Cornwall making his living from drawing and sculpting members of the families who were prepared to give him a roof over his head.

'He had risen to be one of the foremost portrait sculptors in London but ended his days a penniless vagrant in a paupers' hospital in Redruth' wrote Mary Martin, the celebrated Tamar valley artist who became fascinated by Burnard as a young student. She compiled her thesis around his life which was later published by the Lodenek Press (Cornish publishers from Padstow) in 1978 under the title of *'A Wayward Genius – Neville Northey Burnard, Cornish Sculptor 1818 – 1878'* and is a wonderful detailed account of his work and his private life. Mary Martin is not the only Cornish person to become so intrigued by Burnard. Charles Causley, the poet from Launceston, wrote a poem entitled *'A Short Life of Neville Northey Burnard'*. It begins:

Here lived Burnard who with his finger's bone
Broke syllables of light from the moorstone,
Spat on the genesis of dust and clay
Rubbed with huge hands the blinded eyes of day,
And through the seasons of the talking sun
Walked, calm as God, the fields of Altarnun.

Pencrebar, Trematon Castle, Port Eliot and Place. So different, yet with similarities mostly to do with their Cornishness. Each of them holds memories for me as well as filling a place in Cornish history. I believe that this is true even of the house of the least architectural importance – Pencrebar. If you need to know its place in history ask any Methodist or Liberal from South East Cornwall who lived and prayed and canvassed in the first half of the twentieth-century.

The richness of Cornwall in its great places of beauty, its houses, its gardens and its people will never stop intriguing me.

THREE FAVOURITE PLACES OF WORSHIP

CORNWALL abounds with beautiful and unusual churches, some of them are grand and imposing like Truro Cathedral and the carved granite church at Launceston, but my favourite places of worship in Cornwall are small, somewhat remote and all are near water. These three are St Winnow on the River Fowey, the chapel at Halton Quay on the Tamar and St Enodoc on the rugged north coast.

St Winnow Church

It does not matter whether you go on a grey winter's day or a bright shining one, there is something so unique about the setting and the atmosphere that it would be impossible not to fall under the spell. The little grey church is surrounded by slate engraved grave stones, the Fowey River wends its way round the banks of the grave yard and the wooded slopes on the opposite bank give an added dimension.

A L Rowse wrote in *The Little Land of Cornwall*: '*Everywhere (in Cornwall) the river valleys are exquisite, deep and winding – stand in the churchyard of St Winnow on the riverbank of Fowey – the old grey church of the Saint behind you, complete with bench-ends, rood screen, medieval heraldic windows – and look across to the Arthurian wood of Lantyne and down river to the turn towards the open haven of Fowey, the tide running up the channel with a fresh breeze from the sea, invisible but making its presence felt.*'

There is a great sense of peace in that churchyard, a kind of holiness that seems to come from centuries of hope, faith and prayer. Standing by the church, looking out over the river the first time I visited the church I kept whispering to myself: 'This must be the most beautiful place in the world!'

Whenever I have returned I have been afraid that I might be disenchanted, that the magic of the place might have gone and that I had been imagining it all but this has never been the case. It is always tranquil and refreshing.

Inside the little church the atmosphere and beauty is just as strong and comforting. There are some beautiful and ancient carved bench ends and bright and intriguing stained glass windows. The rood screen was carefully restored by Edmund Sedding in 1907 and is one of the few remaining originals in Cornwall.

The uniqueness of St Winnow probably lies in the fact that the church is so secluded although the vicarage and a grand old farmhouse lie close by. Otherwise there is not a sound of modern traffic only the occasional chug of a boat engine, making its way up river on a high tide or the sound of voices wafting across the water from the woods opposite.

St Enodoc

Each year I make a pilgrimage to St Enodoc with a friend of mine. Each year we sit on the bench above the little church, with its crooked spire, and watch the breaking waves beyond and the blue, blue sea and wide sky above. Once this little church was quite literally buried by sand. Now it has become a place of special interest particularly since Sir John Betjeman the Poet Laureate was buried there. The slate stone that marks his grave is most intricately carved. I like to think of the day when he was brought in his coffin to the graveyard carried through driving rain on a typically Cornish day. For, as we all know, to love Cornwall truly you must learn to love the rain. John Betjeman certainly loved Cornwall and managed to conjure up the true atmosphere of the North Coast so well for so many in his poems – as in these two extracts:

On Wadebridge Station what a breath of sea
Scented the Camel Valley! Cornish air,
Soft Cornish rains, and silence after steam ...
As out of Derry's stable came the brake
To drag us up those long, familiar hills,
Past haunted woods and oil-lit farms and on
To far Trebetherick by the sounding sea!
John Betjeman

ST ENODOC: one of the glories of North Cornwall.

Come on, Come on! This hillock hides the spire,
Now that one and now none. As winds about
The burnished path through lady's finger, thyme
And bright varieties of saxifrage,
So grows the tinny tenor faint or loud
And all things draw towards St Enodoc.
John Betjeman

Halton Quay

We used to live just above Halton Quay. Its little white chapel sits just by the wide River Tamar which is tidal here.

Once the building was a coal store, next to it the lime kilns burned at night. This was a quay full of activity a hundred years ago. All the rich produce of the Tamar valley fields: fruit, vegetable and flowers, were brought to this point, loaded on to river barges and sent down to Plymouth Market. The goods were brought by horse and cart or loaded on to mules or donkeys.

At that time the Tamar River was similar to today's motorways with every kind of traffic, both for pleasure and for business, making its way up the river. This was the time of the lucrative mines producing vast quantities of copper ore, and all the paraphernalia of the mining business. Now Halton Quay has reverted to more peaceful activities – the salmon fish netting still takes place here – and a canoeing enterprise has recently started from this point – it is wonderful to see both old and young people setting off up the river silently paddling their way up to the higher reaches of the waterway – discovering the river's life in the best possible way.

Recently I took a friend of mine to see Halton Quay. She had been very ill and worried for weeks. We sat by the river, it was high tide, and as the sun began to sink the yellow light splashed across the water and wooded banks by Pentillie Castle. Not a word was spoken. Later she told me that Halton Quay on that perfect summer's evening had been a better tonic than any medicine or therapy.

When we used to live above Halton Quay, on summer's evenings, we could hear the sound of people singing wafting up the valley. This was the little congregation gathered outside the chapel on the grassy slope vigorously singing the hymns for evensong. These services are held regularly during the summer months.

SIR John Betjeman.

Like St Winnow or St Enodoc I never go to Halton Quay without being newly surprised by the atmosphere and beauty.

THE River Lynher below Cadsonbury – still referred to as Lynher or St German's River.

THE LYNHER

RUN, run,' said my brother. 'The first one to the top wins two shillings and sixpence.' There were four of us, all under twelve years of age, and we were struggling through the bracken to the top of Cadsonbury an old Iron Age Fort.

The monetary prize was offered by our grandfather but the real prize was the reaching of the peak and to sit, breathless from the climb, scarred with scratches from bramble and bracken and to gaze down on the glistening River Lynher.

This was the playground of my youth – nowhere else do I feel so nostalgic for those balmy days of my childhood. We would walk down from my grandfather's house, Pencrebar, on the outskirts of Callington, through the woods and thick rhododendron drives to New Bridge. There was little traffic then – this was in the early 1950s and what traffic there was gave us plenty of time to stand back on one of the little enclaves of the bridge to let the cars or horses pass. Just by New Bridge was a blacksmith. My aunt Sally ran a riding stables at Pencrebar. She kept about ten or fifteen ponies and horses in the Victorian stable block at Pencrebar and we would help her ride or lead the horses down to the blacksmith to have them re-shod. Nothing could be more fascinating to me than to watch the expertise of the blacksmith with his heavy leather apron, divided up the middle, as he lifted the horses' legs, carefully trimmed back their hooves then fitted the smouldering hot iron shoe to the hoof, returning it to the hot coals to hit it in to the right shape.

The sound of the beating of the iron and the mixture of smells of burning hoof, the coal fire, the horse's sweet scent, were so strong that they stay in the memory long after word or facts have disappeared. It was the blacksmith's confidence in his expertise that always impressed me. He never seemed to worry about a slightly skittish horse – with a firm gentle voice and hand he could quieten any fears the animal had and then expect to gain near perfect behaviour. If there were many horses to be shod we would take a pasty and sit by the river watching it rush by with the background sounds and smells.

Other days – and of course they were always sun-shining days like childhood memories often are – we would walk down river to where the islands were. Between the islands there were little bridges so that we could scamper from one island to the other and then claim them as our very own. Further down river there was a small weir and then Clapper Bridge. This was a great place to play a form of Pooh Sticks – each of us choosing a particular twig or small branch dropping it over one side of the bridge and then rushing to see whose came out first the other side.

Just by Clapper Bridge is the old entrance to the fine manor house of Newton Ferrers for many years the home of the Abdy family. When I was a child Lady Diana Abdy was one of the most glamorous and loved figures of the district. A very beautiful woman, she gave a lot of her time and her energy to the surrounding community. She also designed a beautiful water garden going down the grounds surrounding the house (built in 1697). After a terrible fire, when half the house was burned to the ground, one wing was never restored. It had an eerie but awe-inspiring feeling about it – it always seemed shut away from the outside world, hidden, secluded, shunning contact.

Some years ago when I asked Sir Valentine Abdy if I could interview him for a book I was writing, he adamantly refused saying he wanted to keep the house and ground of Newton Ferrers as private as possible. He certainly succeeded, for only a few indigenous people have known about the house and marvelled at its setting above the River Lynher.

Charles Henderson in his book *Old Cornish Bridges* wrote: '*No part of inland Cornwall is more beautiful or less known than the hundred of East Wivelshire (this was the land between Tamar and Fowey) through which the Lynher wends its 27 miles.*' No river can be fully appreciated without knowing its beginning – the Lynher begins its life in the parish of Altarnun and its name is derived from Lyn-hir (long lake) said to be due to its long straight course. So, like so many rivers and streams, the Lynher starts its life on Bodmin Moor and then flows through the magnificent woods at Trebartha then passes on through a sixteenth century country bridge on the road from Launceston to Liskeard then on to Bathpool, Rilla Mill and so to Linkinhorne and Callington's New Bridge and Clapper Bridge and on to the bridge at Pillaton Mill. It is not until Notter Bridge beyond Saltash that the river becomes tidal.

In its journey the river runs through land that encompasses all of the history of Cornwall – through a centre of the tin industry, by granite quarries, farm land, and under bridges used by Roundheads and Cavaliers in the Civil War. Charles I was said to have crossed New Bridge at Callington in 1644 after his hard-won victory at Lostwithiel. The fishery rights were important – in 1669 Sir John Coryton Bart, rented the fishery of the Lynher from the Duchy Manor of Trematon for thirteen shillings and four pence a year.

Charles Henderson described the stages that belong to the lives of rivers – *'First, there is the moorland cradle; then a childhood spent tumbling and laughing over the boulders; next comes youth among green pastures and after that manhood in a deep luxuriant valley of its own creating, harnessed to some industry or other. Old age comes at last with a broad estuary up which the flowing tides come daily to escort the river to the sea.'*

I am lucky enough to live in a house that overlooks the last stages of the River Lynher. This seems to me particularly fortuitous when I should have so many childhood memories of the earlier stages of the river. In almost every room in the house where I live I can see the tidal estuary of the River Lynher. I can watch daily 'The flowing tides – escort the river to the sea'. When the tide is out there is a solemnity and a peacefulness to the mud banks of the wide waters. The light changes constantly to add new dimensions so that the view is never the same.

Herons, shelduck, oystercatchers and curlew give the background music and the movement. On the opposite banks we can see the village of Antony and hear the church bells ring across the water. The great houses of Antony and Ince Castle guard these final stretches to the sea. It is a grand and serenely beautiful ending to the eternal life of this river which has been so much part of *my* life.

LADY ASTOR dancing on the Hoe.

THE HOE

IDEFY anyone driving or walking for the first time from the narrow historic streets of the Barbican up on to the great vista of Plymouth Hoe not to be greatly impressed. The wide expanse of the Sound with Drake's Island placed so picturesquely in its midst, the breakwater, the curving hills of Mount Edgcumbe on the Cornish side, the cliffs at Jennycliff Bay on the Devon side and on a clear day the Eddystone Lighthouse way out on the horizon combine together to make a most splendid sight. I often wish I could have seen the Plymouth Pier, such a feature of life on The Hoe, demolished during the war.

Nowadays, you are more likely to watch the Roscoff ferry arriving and leaving but it is not difficult at all to imagine the great warships of times past making a triumphant entrance to the harbour and to picture the crowds awaiting the return of valiant sailors from adventurous and daring voyages.

Plymouth has known the need for fortifications for hundreds of years. During the reign of Edward I in the twelfth century there were over three hundred ships gathered in Plymouth Sound. It was recorded as the earliest gathering of a national fleet and the first local participation in national maritime affairs on a large scale. This fleet was bound for Guinea to demand the restoration of the King's rights.

In 1346 ships were sent to assist Edward besiege Calais, and Plymouth dispatched twenty-six vessels manned by six hundred men. The first recorded invasion of Plymouth was by the French in the fourteenth century but the most famous of all the attacks during these so called 'private wars' was when the Bretons invaded